PRAISE FOR *STRAY LATITUDES*

T0246743

"In this charming and succinct poetry collection by writer Dan Leach, 'faith may end in the heart, but it begins in the feet.' *Stray Latitudes,* as the title suggests, harnesses the chaos wrought by well-meaning attempts to manage and order human life. Attention to what's surreal, menacing, and strange is offered to us without the poet losing hold of what's sweet and tender. A genuine gift.

I'm thankful to live in a world where poems like Leach's beckon, sweaty—tearful, resisting all the right answers. Saturated in discovery and disruption, this collection begs to be read on a porch somewhere, somewhere poems call us home, insisting next time, 'ask for the world.'"

—LAUREN K. CARLSON, author of
Animals I Have Killed

"*Stray Latitudes* embraces the fleeting movements of human experience. Life moves fast here, building the loop we'll ride in a nameless cul-de-sac, pausing to hear and ask the questions we'll struggle to answer. These poems speak to us, say this is who we are, this is where we are now—somewhere in the space between the natural world that is living and the dying around us, and the life-drunk and the dead-sobriety that punctuates man's destruction—and they say this is where we'll be back again, trying to remember. What is so refreshing here is the acceptance, the confidence of a voice that understands the agency of memory, how we live in it, and with it. Because it, too, like 'everyone, even God, must be tested.' And that's where light of these poems come from. It is such a brilliant collection!"

—RAY MCMANUS, author of
The Last Saturday in America and *Punch*

"*Stray Latitudes* is a book interested in the big questions: how to live, how to love, how to keep faith in the face of doubt. Leach approaches these questions aslant, transforming the ordinary world around him into a place mysterious and full of wonder. A bulldozer becomes a lion; a garage turns into a cave; cigarette smoke curls through the air 'like a song / written in a tongue / long since dead.' It's hard to blend wry humor and total sincerity—but Leach does it seamlessly. Small-town South Carolina springs to life in each line. Each moment is meaningful, a microcosm of a much larger world, captured with careful detail and enormous heart."

—KATIE PRINCE, author of
Tell This to the Universe

"Dan Leach writes a hole into the wind. Through stumble after get up after stumble after love after stumble after dream his poems do the creatively impossible: they achieve balance without symmetry. But that is only the beginning. The real sparks fly when he turns the poem on himself and the world and disturbs the balance without the conversation crashing into personal rhetoric. No wonder he frightens all the half-truths we don't know how to live without. *Stray Latitudes* is a brilliant debut."

—BARRETT WARNER, author of
Why Is It So Hard to Kill You?

"*Stray Latitudes* opens mid-pandemic, immersed in eerie quiet of suburbia where new construction has halted, and bulldozers sleep like 'a pack of tired lions.' Leach gracefully braids issues of capitalism, global warming, sprawl, and loneliness where the weird panic of the present becomes permanent as 'the world moved inside.' In the latter part of the book, Leach explores memory, loss, and childhood, creating an atmosphere you can taste. Are all memories poems? Leach leads us down the abandoned alley, playing a 90's alt-rock soundtrack, smoking Reds, and making us believe that 'what you loved could never die.'"

—NATALIE SOLMER, Editor-in-Chief at
The Indianapolis Review

STRAY LATITUDES

Come a long, long way from nowhere
With armor made from nothing
But some songs I learned along the way
from some strangers

from "I Want Blood" by Water Liars

STRAY LATITUDES

POEMS

DAN LEACH

The TRP Southern Poetry Breakthrough Series:
South Carolina

TRP: THE UNIVERSITY PRESS OF SHSU
HUNTSVILLE, TEXAS 77340

Library of Congress Cataloging-in-Publication Data

Names: Leach, Dan, 1985- author.
Title: Stray latitudes : poems / Dan Leach.
Other titles: TRP Southern poetry breakthrough series.
Description: First edition. | Huntsville : TRP: The University Press of
  SHSU, [2024] | Series: TRP Southern poetry breakthrough series: South
  Carolina
Identifiers: LCCN 2023033967 (print) | LCCN 2023033968 (ebook) | ISBN
  9781680033830 (paperback) | ISBN 9781680033847 (ebook)
Subjects: LCSH: Suburban life--South Carolina--Social conditions--21st
  century--Poetry. | Group identity--Southern States--Poetry. | Southern
  States--Social life and customs--21st century--Poetry. | Southern
  States--Civilization--Poetry. | LCGFT: Poetry.
Classification: LCC PS3612.E212755 S87 2024 (print) | LCC PS3612.E212755
  (ebook) | DDC 811/.6--dc23/eng/20230725
LC record available at https://lccn.loc.gov/2023033967
LC ebook record available at https://lccn.loc.gov/2023033968

FIRST EDITION

Author photo courtesy: Hannah Leach
Cover design by Cody Gates, Happenstance Type-O-Rama
Interior design by Maureen Forys, Happenstance Type-O-Rama

Printed and bound in the United States of America

TRP: The University Press of SHSU
Huntsville, Texas 77340
texasreviewpress.org

The TRP Southern Poetry Breakthrough Series
Series Editor: J. Bruce Fuller

The TRP Southern Poetry Breakthrough Series highlights a debut full-length collection by emerging authors from each state in the southern United States.

BOOKS IN THIS SERIES:

South Carolina: Dan Leach, *Stray Latitudes*

West Virginia: Kelly McQuain, *Scrape the Velvet from Your Antlers*

Arkansas: James Dunlap, *Heaven's Burning Porch*

Florida: Caridad Moro-Gronlier, *Tortillera*

Georgia: Erin Ganaway, *The Waiting Girl*

Texas: Lindsay Illich, *Rile & Heave*

Louisiana: Chris Hannan, *Alluvial Cities*

Mississippi: Noel Polk, *Walking Safari: Or, The Hippo Highway*

North Carolina: Sally Stewart Mohney, *Low Country, High Water*

Tennessee: William Kelley Woolfitt, *Beauty Strip*

For Hannah

CONTENTS

PART III: ASK FOR THE WORLD

PART I

SOME WEATHER IS PERMANENT

CONSTRUCTION SITE

For C. Vann Woodward

Beyond our street, bulldozers
rest in the empty lot, their blades
lowered in the morning rain.
They have not moved in months,
not since last spring, when having
cleared the last of the ponderosas
they lay down—a pack of tired lions,
stomachs swollen, content to sleep
in the mud and never rise again.

BLUE HERON IN RETENTION POND

He stomachs the empty hours, waiting
        for what is under the surface

to draw near. Saint of the subjunctive,
        standing in the rain, desiring

everything while expecting nothing.
        He works in possibilities: to snatch

a shadow from the murk, to retreat
        into the sky, still alone, still alive,

a pilgrim caught between two gods.

HEAT WAVE

Then came the summer
the creeks went dry
and everyone's grass turned
the color of bone.
Streets became graveyards
and even the pool
with its pale green promise
yawned in the distance
like a forgotten church.

The world moved inside.

It is never easy to live
in the gap between
what you once had
and what you now want.

Memory, that virus.

But the man on the TV
said not to worry,
all weather is temporary.

The man said one day
we would wake up
and the world we knew
would be right where
it had always been.

We believed him,
eating banana popsicles
and napping under fans,
killing time
with all the books
we'd been too busy
to read back when
the world was cool.

For a while waiting
feels like waiting.
Then it feels like living.

We did everything
we were supposed to do,
but the heat refused to leave.
The heat got hotter.
It stayed for weeks
then it stayed for years.
The man on the TV
who was wrong
about everything
got replaced by another
man who said some
weather is permanent.

THE GADSDEN INDEX

Any flag will change if you watch it
long enough. You were once a sporadic
flash of dandelion, the odd man's stand,
present but fading on some porch
in need of paint. Now you strike out
from everywhere, a cancer of coiled
resentment, attacking the heart of my town
as if it wasn't you who once believed
the only unpardonable sin is treading
on a neighbor too weary to rise up.

TWO CAR GARAGE

At night they were caves:
some father (not yours) working
alone by fire.

MORNING RUN

Among the crabgrass
of a dirt path
only runners use now,
a dead owl, splayed
in pale surrender,
black eyes open
and flung skyward
asking, not why,
but why here.

It is too cold
to stop, but I carry
his question with me,
tell the black eyes
of my mind
it will be different
next time around.

RECURRING DREAM OF EX

Again the one
where it is the darkest
night of the year
and we are dancing
in the center
of a frozen lake,
dancing as children do,
no steps, no time,
all limbs and heart,
the bone-deep refusal
to let go, to forget
for even a second
your confession
from our final
night together—
I only believe
in beginnings.

ILLUSTRATED BIBLE STORIES FOR CHILDREN

Young children make
the best agnostics.
They remind us,
the inoculated,
how to seek.

As the father
of four healthy non-believers,
three girls and a boy,
I am constantly encouraged
to be less certain.

Mornings we eat pancakes.
I read stories from The Bible.
They ask for the strange ones.
Moses and the burning bush.
Lazarus come back.
Anything with angels.

My kids listen,
but nothing I read
is automatically true.
Everyone, even God,
must be tested.

They ask questions,
and some mornings
my answers suffice.

Why did Jesus have to die?
To show us that death is not the end.

If Peter loved Christ, why did he deny him?
No amount of love means you're not afraid.

Will there be animals in heaven?
Many.

Other days we drift
together into cruel ambiguities.

If God knew the serpent
wanted to trick Eve,
why didn't He stop it?

If Christ is love,
and love wins in the end,
what is the deal with Hell?

What if the whole movement,
right down to the resurrection,
is based on a mistake? Even worse,
what if it's based on a lie?

These are not sad mornings,
but we do admit together:
this world has grown sick
with secrets and half-lights.

Still their questions
are worth more to me
than all the prayers

of all the saints,
since saints have reached
the end of searching.

The only lesson
I hope to teach them
is that doubt is its own
kind of worship,
and that the water
you drink as you wander
this desert of unknowing
must always be love.

COLD MOON

Maybe you are a dead rock
making a name off stolen light,
but I never minded pretenders.

I once met a writer
who introduced himself
as "an original mind."
He had the smile
of a dependable switchblade.
He offered me
all of his secrets
for the price of a book.

The first girl I ever loved
was a punk with blue hair.
She stole glue from the art room
and gave herself a mohawk.
When I asked for her name,
she said, "It used to be Katherine.
Now it's Dani Cyanide."

When I grow up,
I want to be a good liar.

DENTIST FRIEND

When I asked him
how much
he would charge
to pull a hot tooth,

he looked at me
like my name
was Uncle Trash.

I had to pretend
I was joking.

I had to remember
he was a Christian
from Ohio,
well-respected in his trade.

SOBRIETY

I.

I tried to be less dead today:
out of the grave and into the garden.

By noon I was thirsty and called
Sam with the beard from the meeting.

Sam says drinking is a window
that lets you look out past yourself.

If Sam is right (and he always is)
then sobriety must be a mirror.

All morning I stared at my face.
I didn't think much of the view.

II.

All these fractious early hours—
they used to seem like such friends.

I made some coffee and ate an orange.
I smoked cigarettes and read a novel.

I went for a run and did some sit ups.
I made a salad and wrote a letter.

But stability is its own kind of fog,
and this dark chocolate barely works.

Please Lord don't remind me
this day is one fight at a time.

III.

I can't tell you about the drinking
unless I tell you about the past.

I can't tell you about the past
because then you'd see me shake.

Sam says shaking is the point:
feed the fever until it breaks.

But why does drinking seem inevitable
now that the morning light is gone?

Why have I only read of resurrections
in certain books I got for free?

SILVERLEAF

The two girls
smoking grapevine
at the bottom
of a dried-up creek
might stay
forever laughing
in the memory
of the boy
who walked
through the woods
and heard their voices
just in time to turn
and see the plumes
from the earth
rising like a song
written in a tongue
long since dead.

IVORY-BILLED WOODPECKER IN DISCARDED
REFRIGERATOR BEHIND HARRIS TEETER

Say the red crest blazed
as it left that old box,
a strange fire spit
at the horizon,
first a ghost
among the sweetgums,
then a distant flapping,
finally nothing.
Forget your history.
Better to be quiet
in woods nobody visits
thinking, Good Lord,
all memories are poems.

PART II

NO ONE HERE HAS EVER BEEN LONELY

OPEN HOUSE

The realtor who told us over the phone
that buying a house requires two things—
persistence and vision—now glides smiling
through empty rooms, her braceleted wrists
fluttering in the sunlight like a pair
of desperate sparrows. Everything new,
everything possible, as she tells us the story
of what shape our life might take, here
in Sugar Creek. We listen. We persist
in our envisioning, decorating absence
with makeshift pieces of our future.
How the living room with vaulted ceiling
could be perfect for a Christmas tree.
How the kitchen with the windows
would be nice for kids (if there are kids)
to do homework in natural light.
The realtor says she could see us here.
What she means is that lived life
is still ahead of us, perfectly open,
and that no one has ever felt lonely
in the place where we are standing.

HOME BUYING TIP NO. 17: THE TRUTH ABOUT YARDS

The realtor said, It's true
there's not much yard here,
but I'm a parent myself
and let me tell you—
children don't need space.
If they want trees,
they will dream them up.
When they need a river,
a river will come,
and you will look outside
and see them sailing off
into forever. A good fence
and a little bit of grass—
let them envision the rest.

THE YEAR AFTER YOUR FATHER DIES

They said expect numbness and I thought it'd feel like being drunk.
Instead it came the other way—precarious as the waltz of sobriety.

Not like driving the street where your old house was.
More like walking through woods where no home will ever be.

It is not the key cut for a lock you can't remember.
Rather the old claw-hammer held together by tape.

Most nights it's like a three-legged dog running home
through the rain. And here you thought you could name this.

FELL BEAST SNARLS

I want my childhood back.
Not to live it again,
just to kick it
in its stomach
and say, *Tell me
how that feels.*

THE DREAMS OF CERTAIN SAINTS

There are people
whose dreams are doors
to the other side,
sleepers who do not sleep
so much as wander
through the wild gardens
of their strange god.

One called me yesterday
from halfway across the world.
She said, *The Lord gave me a word*
and I believe it belongs to you.
She said, *I was walking*
on a frozen lake and I looked
down through the ice and saw
a boat on the bottom.
She said, *The lake is your life.*
The boat, your heart.

Another time she warned me
not to trust men with blue eyes
for at least a month.
She said, *Promise me*
you will be careful.
She called a week later
and said, *You're safe now.*

The strangest of all was
the night she called me

and said, *I know you feel unseen,*
but there is one coming
who is the end of all loneliness.
No one spoke after this,
but no one hung up either.

If I find it hard to believe
in places other than here,
that does not mean I will
ignore her calls. Silence
is no place for the weary,
and it has been years since
I have had a dream of my own.

HOME BUYING TIP NO. 38: SWEAT EQUITY

The realtor pointed at the place
where a patio could be.
Said, You two imagine
how much this property
will be worth in five years,
if you are not afraid
to put some work in.
That is what I would do
if I were in your position:
sweat, sweat, sweat.

AN EMPTY TOMB IS ITS OWN KIND OF ARCHITECTURE

If you mean to walk far
with a god who stays gone,
consider the possibility
that you have lost your mind.

And maybe you have
since delusions are like dreams:
you know you're in one when
you swear you're not in one.

Maybe what you call a voice
is nothing more than a thought,
and what you call Christ
is your fear of being forgotten.

If this is the truth
(and we all want the truth),
then the road to your god
is a bridge to nowhere.

But to believe is to stand
inside of an empty tomb
and say to its silence,
I know who keeps you.

INSTRUCTIONS FROM STORE MANAGER OF ORANGE JULIUS ON THE DAY THE MALL CLOSED DOWN

If you sit around thinking
about where all this is going
you will never do anything at all

CLOSING (OR: THERE IS NO CREEK IN SUGAR CREEK)

surviving here
is knowing
how to walk
across fields
over rivers
always moving
never leaving
the place
you call
your yard

BETWEEN HOMES

Out where porch lights carve
a hard border between the end
of our new yard and a muddy run
of skeleton homes, a possum
skulks low through the lilyturf,
pale face kind but unsmiling,
cautious, as if warned that leaving
darkness is a dangerous move.
She is not alone. Her back flattens
to carry the world: five joeys,
all black eyed and glinting,
as when broken glass woos
the moon from wet pavement.
On seeing me, she slips back
into the grass, rejoining the night
with an exile's measured ease.
I would let her stay forever,
but I am the stranger here,
and it is possible the light
of my house is no light at all.

PART III

ASK FOR THE WORLD

FIST FIGHT WITH OLDER SIBLING

blood back then
tasted like pennies

it was only red
in your mouth

once dried
on your shirt

it looked brown
as any mud

closer in color
to your brother's hair

remember
you are remembered

as the one
who always lost

hate it but
remember anyway

how closely love
walked with cruelty

how when he said
stay down

he meant
the opposite

TRANSPLANT

Here   is a poem
Here   is a poem
Here   is a poem
Here   is a poem

Here   is a hoem
Here   is a hoem
Here   is a hoem
Here   is a hoem

Here   is a home
Here   is a home
Here   is a home
Here (at last) is a home

WHEN I WAS A CHILD I THREW ROCKS AT THE MOON

i was born small   i grew up small
i have desires so small   no one else
can see them

here is one   only you know
when i was a child
there was a field   behind my house
nights i would stand in it
and throw rocks at   the moon

i had asked my mother   where you live
she said   up there
and pointed to the sky
then i knew the score
the sky   was just a window

between your house   and mine
and to get you to come   outside
i had break the glass

everything has changed
since   then
i went by that field
the other day
the creek was   dried up
and the house was   gone
yet little piles of rocks
still covered the   ground
like old abandoned   fires

THE FIFTH OF JULY

Last night left sawdust
all over our cul-de-sac:
Cherry Bombs, still new.

CUL-DE-SAC

Alex from across the street
led me to a cul-de-sac,
out to where a street-lamp
carved a circle of light
on the rain-slick pavement.
In that circle, a gray lump,
still, no bigger than a fist.
It's a bat, he said. *And it's dead.*

I drew closer. Little bones
in the wings, a silent pink face.
To see him meant knowing
in your heart: it should not
be like this. I lifted his body
into the light and the wing
was a backlit map with veins
that ran in rivers, countries
carved out in bones. I said,
We have to bury him.

Then the angry mouth,
his teeth in my thumb,
my blood on the pavement.
That is how it should have been:
Alex and I in the cul-de-sac,
laughing like fools, and him,
somewhere up and somewhere else,
dancing, dancing, dancing.

MAP OF THE NEIGHBORHOOD DRAWN BY EMILY KOSA ON THE BACK OF A CHURCH BULLETIN AND SOLD FOR A QUARTER (OR: THE MOMENT I REALIZED I WOULD BE BORED FOREVER IF I DIDN'T TRY TO WRITE POEMS)

There was a monster
where Liam's house should have been.
I liked it that way.

THE FIRST TWENTY-FOUR YEARS OF MY LIFE

I saw a girl at the end of a long dirt road. She had a smeared white dress and dust-covered feet. She had a table and a sign. The table was empty. The sign read, *One Dollar*. I asked what she was selling and she said, *Anything*. I wanted to believe her, but it was too hot to believe in anything, except maybe your own thirst. Sweat leaked out of everything, even my wrists. My tongue, rust. I said, *Anything*? She put her fists on the table. She was completely dry. *Go on*, she said. *Ask*. It was all I could do to reach into my pocket and remove four quarters. I stacked the coins on her table. *One glass of lemonade*, I said. *Ice cubes, if possible*. She looked at the quarters as if they were cursed. She looked at my face like we were ancient enemies. Pocketing my money, she said, *Next time, ask for the world*.

THE PILGRIM

For Matthew Merson

The black bear who passed in front of our cabin
as I sat on the porch trying to remember
what it felt like to be a child and believe in God
paused for a moment before disappearing
into the woods. He regarded me with indifference,
too immersed in his search to register my being.

BETHESDA

Say you are broken because you are waiting
for an angel to arrive and trouble your life
   until your soul sings like it used to.

I wept that prayer for years but never saw any angels.
Only a city of locusts who gorged each night
   on my string of wasted days.

If my past appeared to you it would come wearing a cemetery,
years like the bones of a thousand birds
   swallowed by a grave without a name.

Faith may end in the heart, but it begins in the feet.
If the body can be a key, it can also be a cage.
   Hear: rise, take up thy bed, and walk.

When we leave this city, we will bring our beds with us.
Let us show them to the strangers in the place where we are going.
   Say: but look how the blood has faded.

APPROXIMATION NO. 62

We once found a tabby dead in the street
and buried her in the field behind our house.
Three days later, she was napping in the window.
The field: nothing but an empty grave.

Once we saw a woman with turquoise hair
waltzing naked across our porch.
She wailed *Reset! Reset! Reset!*
until someone (not us) called the police.

Strangest was the Cadillac with no driver
that once circled our street for hours
while a blood moon hung
like an iced plum in the sky.

Forgive this approximation.

What I really want to say is this:
I am thinking tonight of you.
You told me a world without resurrections
isn't worth the story you'd give it.

Back then I rolled my eyes.

AFTER THE SUMMER WE WOULD ONLY WEAR
BLACK CHUCK TAYLORS

came the summer we would only
drink suicides, which was followed by
the summer we would only listen
to *Tigermilk*, which itself faded
into the summer we would only smoke
Marlboro Reds in the empty alley
behind the old Harris Teeter, the one place
where if you closed your eyes
long enough you could pretend
you had never felt this before—the certainty
that what you loved could never die,
and that the moon taking shape
as you smoked your last cigarette,
no matter how long it stayed gone,
would always return to this place

ACKNOWLEDGMENTS

Grateful acknowledgment is made to the publications in which some of these poems first appeared: "Sobriety" in *On the Seawall*; "Silverleaf" and "Fist Fight with Older Sibling" in *Leon Literary Review*; "The Year After Your Father Dies" and "When I Was a Child I Threw Rocks at the Moon" in *Cutleaf*; "Bethesda" and "An Empty Tomb is Its Own Kind of Architecture" in *Mockingbird*; "Between Homes" in *Quarter After Eight;* "The First Twenty-Four Years of My Life" in *Apocalypse Confidential*; "Heat Wave" in *Hawaii Pacific Review*

Thanks to my wife, Hannah Leach, and our children, Reagan, Eisley, Beckett, and Marlow for their bottomless stores of warmth, generosity, and support. Thanks also to the following poets and friends, whose critiques helped shape this book: Ed Skoog, Stephen Hundley, Matthew Meade, Denton Loving, Aaron Strumwasser, Katie Prince, Jason Storms, Natalie Solmer, Lauren Carlson, Phil Canipe, and Matthew Merson.

ABOUT THE AUTHOR

Dan Leach has published work in *Copper Nickel*, *The Southwest Review*, and *The Sun*. He has two collections of short fiction: *Floods and Fires* (University of North Georgia, 2017) and *Dead Mediums* (Trident Press, 2022). He holds an MFA from Warren Wilson and currently teaches writing at Charleston Southern University. *Stray Latitudes* is his first collection of poetry.